ANIMALS
OBSERVED

ANIMALS OBSERVED

A LOOK AT ANIMALS IN ART

Dorcas MacClintock

CHARLES SCRIBNER'S SONS • NEW YORK
Maxwell Macmillan Canada • Toronto
Maxwell Macmillan International
New York • Oxford • Singapore • Sydney

ACKNOWLEDGMENTS

The idea for a book about animals in art was sparked when the late Charlotte Ball Seymour suggested to Caroline Rollins of the Yale University Art Gallery that I take part in a 1985 lecture series, *Creatures of Paradise*. A year later Professors Mary Etta Hight and John A. W. Kirsch sponsored a similar lecture at the annual meeting of the American Society of Mammalogists in Madison, Wisconsin.

William K. Sacco, chief photographer at Yale Peabody Museum, shared my enthusiasm and skillfully captured the spirit of each animal—modeled, carved, painted, and drawn—that came into his studio.

Veronique Fromanger Des Cordes and Jacques-Chalom Des Cordes, devoted to the sculptor and his work, generously provided for the use of photographs from their catalog raisonné, *Rembrandt Bugatti* (Paris: Les Éditions de L'Amateur, 1987).

I am most grateful to Betty Muirden, reference librarian at the Yale Center for British Art, for her unstinting assistance in requesting permissions from museums and galleries and for tracking down biographical information on several lesser-known artists. At the Paul Mellon Centre for Studies in British Art in London, Mrs. Evelyn Newby kindly guided my pursuit of the chestnut horse *Whistlejacket*.

When permission to include another horse was unobtainable, it was Charles Scribner III, art historian and publisher, who managed to lay a hand on the beautiful gray stallion that appears on page 49.

Charles Scribner's Sons Books for Young Readers
Macmillan Publishing Company
866 Third Avenue, New York, NY 10022

Maxwell Macmillan Canada, Inc.
1200 Eglinton Avenue East, Suite 200
Don Mills, Ontario M3C 3N1

Macmillan Publishing Company is part of the Maxwell Communication Group of Companies.

First Edition   10 9 8 7 6 5 4 3 2 1
Printed in the United States of America
Book design by Vikki Sheatsley

Library of Congress Cataloging-in-Publication Data
MacClintock, Dorcas
    Animals observed : a look at animals in art / Dorcas MacClintock. —1st ed.
        p.   cm.   Includes index.
    Summary: A collection of drawings, paintings, and sculptures depicting a variety of animals, including giraffes, elephants, zebras, squirrels, dogs, cats, and horses. Discusses the artists and the animals they observed.
    ISBN 0-684-19323-X
    1. Animals in art—Juvenile literature.   2. Art—Juvenile literature.
    [1. Animals in art.   2. Art appreciation.]   I. Title.
N7660.M25   1993   704.9'432—dc20   91-36795

To G. Evelyn Hutchinson
1903–1991

Distinguished biologist and friend.
Knowing of this book, he counseled,
"Be sure to tell something about the animals."

CONTENTS

INTRODUCTION

Animals Observed is a gathering of drawings, paintings, and sculptures of animals, all of them mammals. Neither a Noah's Ark of animals, two of every sort, nor an alphabet of animals, the book consists of animal images whose appeal is their own.

The animals themselves were *well observed*. They are portrayed both lovingly and skillfully by artists who had in common an intense interest in animals and who observed with empathy.

Empathy takes various forms. A closeness, an awareness, a respect for, or a love of—all are definitions of empathy. With empathy comes an understanding so intimate that an animal's feelings, thoughts, and motives are interpreted. It is empathy that imparts life and individuality and enables an artist to capture on canvas or in clay the essence of an animal.

My pursuit of animals in art began some years ago, with an invitation to take part in an art-gallery series called Creatures of Paradise. Although it meant treading on the hallowed turf of art history, it offered the chance to celebrate some of the animals in art that I find compelling. And so the gathering of animal images began, a pleasant pursuit to which there is seemingly no end.

Because my life is much involved with animals, those that are my particular favorites—giraffes, zebras, elephants, raccoons and their relatives, squirrels, and of course dogs, cats, and horses—occupy more pages than other animals that may be your particular favorites. A book on animals in art, of necessity, consists of many more omissions than inclusions.

Many of the animals in this book are portrayed with realism, represented as they actually appeared, accurate in outline, body contour, and color. But even in realism, the eyes and hands of the artist select and modify, with acute perception and, often, with personal sensitivity.

The art of hunters—prehistoric cave painters, carvers of the Far North, and naturalists with artistic flair—is included here, too, for it has both authority and appeal. And it, too, involves empathy and a kind of love for the animal.

Most of the plates that illustrate natural history volumes of a century or more ago, when there was avid interest in science, were intended to show what a particular animal looked like, to record its shape, color, and markings. But many of them are works of art. The animal depicted was well observed and the pose natural and expressive of its character.

Some of the images are the work of impressionists, artists who sought to record an actual moment in time, what the eye saw in a glance. Impressionism, even in clay and bronze, is often sketchy. Details are left for the viewer to supply. An ear may be left off, or barely indicated. Volume is sometimes sacrificed for surface vibrations of light and shadow. On canvas a leg may be left unpainted. Yet feeling and sentiment are conveyed in the artist's transient impression. Visual appeal is created and the viewer responds with immediate comprehension.

Other animals were observed with respectful imagination. They are stylized, often with elegant simplicity, and sometimes with humor.

1

OBSERVING ANIMALS

Intense interest in animals has led artists throughout time to specialize, to portray animals as they see them. This form of art requires observing and coming to know the animal portrayed, whether it is a pet rabbit or a rhinoceros. Dogs, cats, horses, even farm animals, are readily found as models. To sketch or sculpt wild animals, however, artists, except for a handful of intrepid artists who were also field naturalists, have had to rely on animals in captivity, at first in menageries and later in zoos.

Among royalty, the keeping of menageries and the exchange of exotic animals as gifts has a long tradition. The zebra that posed for George Stubbs (page 33) and the giraffe that was painted by Jacques-Laurent Agasse (page 23) belonged to British monarchs who were avid menagerie keepers.

Artists themselves have kept animals. Rosa Bonheur filled her studio (*left*) on the rue de l'Ouest in Paris with her animal models, sheep, a goat, a horse, and cats.

In the Zoo

Zoos, established during the nineteenth century, often with a nucleus of animals that came from a private or commercial menagerie, have always attracted artists.

It was late in life when Sir Edwin Landseer was commissioned to do the four lions for the base of Admiral Nelson's Column in Trafalgar Square, London. He had frequented the collection of Ed-

ward Cross, the animal dealer, at Exeter Change in the Strand, and had sketched lions from life there. But finding the newly established London Zoo a far better place to see lions, he went there to sketch. And, for a time, he kept an aged lion, loaned to him by the zoo, in his studio. For nearly a decade Landseer struggled with his huge clay lions that would be cast in bronze.

In the zoo, an artist often sketches or models as zoogoers, curious to see what the artist is seeing, gather about easel or modeling stand. But zoos make provisions for artists, allowing them to come in the early morning, before the zoo opens to the public, and to work where their animal subjects are readily observed. A few fortunate artists have even found studio space in the zoo.

Ugo Mochi often visited the Bronx Zoo in New York. When he was nearly satisfied with his model of a giraffe, the model himself came over for a look.

Rembrandt Bugatti liked to work outdoors, in the Jardin des Plantes in Paris and at the Antwerp Zoo. Once he chose his model, he observed it intently. Then he set to work, quickly covering his wire armature with plasteline.

4

Zoos are places to look for animals in art. On the south facade of the ornate Elephant House at the Bronx Zoo is an Asian elephant by A. Phimister Proctor, shown here as he carves.

FOXES AND WOLVES

Sweden's Bruno Liljefors possessed a sensitivity to animals, as well as a keen eye and visual memory. A painter of landscapes with animals in them, he delighted in watching animals, observing their habits, admiring their expressive body forms, and noting the way they related to their surroundings. Liljefors pronounced animals so wonderfully made that they were perfect, in any position. He painted each animal as an individual.

The red fox, a favorite subject, was an animal he observed often and knew well.

Deep in the woods, in a tangle of shrubs, two foxes have their daytime resting place. The vixen is curled asleep. The dog fox, stretched out with his long brush behind him, is panting. He is clearly annoyed by the chickadees whose persistent scolding calls attention to the foxes' secluded lair.

Although better known as a painter, Charles Marion Russell was also a fine sculptor. The wilderness West was Charley Russell's country. He was sixteen when he left his St. Louis home, bound for Montana Territory. He herded sheep, then worked with a trapper named Jake Hoover. With clay found outside the cabin door, Russell began to model.

Charley Russell liked to carry a ball of beeswax in his pocket. Joining friends at the Silver Dollar Bar, he sat with his hands beneath the table and worked the wax. His cronies tried to guess what animal he was modeling. When the small wax figure appeared on the table, it was the cowboy who had failed to guess its identity who bought the next round of drinks.

The Old West was disappearing. Russell's wife, Nancy, commented that "Charley was here to see the change. He did not like the new; so [he] started to record the old in ink, paint, and clay."

Spontaneity, accuracy of observation, and understanding of the animal are wonderfully combined in this small wax sculpture of a lone gray wolf padding along a trail and hoping to start a jackrabbit from under a sagebrush bush.

Russell saw the wolf vanish in the West, persecuted by trappers and ranchers and often cast as an outlaw. Attitudes toward wolves are changing. Wolves are regarded as having the right to coexist with human beings as part of the natural world. It would please Charley Russell that there are plans to restore the wolf to wilderness areas of Montana.

This small bronze fox, the work of Pierre Jules Mêne, once belonged to the artist Paul Bransom. After Antoine-Louis Barye, Mêne is the best known of the *animaliers*, as a group of French artists who specialized in modeling and carving animals called themselves. Like Barye, Mêne was a careful observer of animals.

Mêne modeled the erect triangular ears and the pointed muzzle of this small canid (member of the dog family) that hunts for field mice and other small rodents and, on occasion, raids a farmer's hen house. Looking at the fox trying to free its leg from a snare, one senses the farmer's approach and hopes he will spare the fox.

The bold simplification of François Pompon's white bear is striking. Sleek and streamlined surfaces impart dignity. No details obscure the solidly rounded body, with its subtle curves of head and neck, and massive, furred paws.

Pompon had a special fondness for bears. For many years this modest, small man with a walrus-like mustache and bushy eyebrows was a carver for the sculptor Auguste Rodin. Pompon did much of the cutting of large blocks of marble, following the forms of Rodin's plaster models.

Pompon's studio in the Montparnasse section of Paris was also a menagerie. The animals he kept were both his friends and his models. The sculptor was convinced that through close contact with them he gained artistic understanding.

Unlike some of the earlier *animalier* artists, Pompon portrayed animals in quiet moods, never fighting or locked in predator-prey struggles. He worked on a small scale and his bronzes attracted little attention.

Often Pompon spent mornings in the Jardin des Plantes, and it must have been there that he saw a polar bear. Pompon's bear, carved from a block of white marble, impressed his artist friends, one of whom insisted he submit *L'Ours Blanc* in place of his own entry in the Salon of 1922.

Pompon's polar bear was acclaimed by critics and art collectors. At last the work of the gentle sculptor was recognized, and his animals, most of them small, highly polished bronzes, came to be coveted.

HIPPOPOTAMUSES

Here is William, the small blue hippopotamus that is a favorite of visitors to the Metropolitan Museum of Art. Modeled some 4,000 years ago in Egypt, the blue faience (glazed earthenware) hippo is an early example of an animal sculpted for its own sake. The Egyptians were keen observers of the natural world. To suggest appropriate habitat, the artist decorated the hippo's blue hide with lotus flowers.

Found in the tomb of the Twelfth Dynasty steward Senbi, the little hippo acquired the name William many centuries later, when his likeness became the talisman of a prominent British family.

In a small bronze group, sculptor Donald Miller suggests the bond between hippo mother and calf. The rainy-season birth of this calf took place on land. But sometimes a calf is born underwater and must paddle hard to the surface for its first breath.

The mother hippo is protective of her calf. She licks, nuzzles, and grooms it with scrapes of her lower incisor teeth. Often the calf nurses underwater, popping to the surface every few seconds for air, then submerging to regain a tight tongue-hold on the teat. Even out of water, the calf suckles with ears folded and nostrils closed.

DOGS

The *Sleeping Bloodhound* is perhaps the most moving and painterly of all Sir Edwin Landseer's dog portraits. The large hound is painted with powerful and broadly handled brush strokes. Wrote a critic for the *Examiner*, a London newspaper, "The animal is dashed in upon the canvas, and lies sleeping there."

In fact, although the impression of sleep is what the artist intended, the dog he painted was not sleeping. The bloodhound Countess was a favorite dog of the artist's friend Jacob Bell. Bell had asked Landseer to paint the bloodhound, but the artist had put off the commission.

Countess met an untimely and tragic death. Her usual sleeping place was the small balcony off her master's bedroom. It was from there that she either lost her balance and fell twenty-five feet to the ground below, or in excitement over her master's return late at night, jumped from the balcony to greet him.

The next day, a Monday, the grieving Jacob Bell took his dead Countess to Landseer's studio and confronted the artist with his failed commission. Landseer took the dog's body, turned to his friend, and said, "Go away. Come on Thursday at two o'clock." When Bell returned three days later the painting had been finished.

The stiffness of limbs, caused in the model by *rigor mortis*, suggests an old dog asleep. Contrasts of light (the comfortable white rug) and dark create a melancholy mood that echoes the artist's sympathy for both dog and master.

The sporting artist Cecil Aldin had a special feel for terriers, those bright-eyed, quick-spirited, sturdy breeds whose roots run deep in the United Kingdom. The name terrier comes from the Latin *terra*, meaning "earth" and refers to the talent these dogs have for wriggling into ground burrows to evict foxes and badgers.

This unkempt little dog is Riley, a wirehaired fox terrier praised in verse by Patrick R. Chalmers in *The Cecil Aldin Book* as quick with "varmints to tackle and 'larn.' "

Like all terriers, Riley has a docked tail. The practice of docking goes back to a time when nobility sought to restrict the owning of hunting dogs, and those who had long-tailed dogs were heavily taxed. Terrier owners soon found that a docked tail made an excellent handle for retrieving a dog from a burrow.

The writer Albert Payson Terhune claimed that "a dog is a dog, but a collie is—a collie." Certainly the collies that lived at Sunnybank, Terhune's New Jersey estate, were not ordinary dogs. Generations have grown up loving the accounts of the loyalty and bravery of the Sunnybank collies.

Paul Bransom was the illustrator of several of Terhune's short stories, as well as his books *Lad of Sunnybank* and *Gray Dawn*. Often he visited Sunnybank to sketch from life.

According to Terhune, life at Sunnybank was "wondrous pleasant." There was a lake for swimming and, in front of the big fireplace, a "deliciously comfortable old rug" on which the collies could lie, shoulder to shoulder on cold wintry nights. Paul Bransom sketched this collie, a mahogany sable with white frill and collar, on the wisteria-covered veranda that the collies and their people enjoyed on summer days.

Sir Edwin Landseer painted many of Queen Victoria's pets. Sometimes he portrayed them in groups. Landseer was said to have gained royal favor through his own fondness for Scotland's terrier breeds. In this Buckingham Palace setting, mood is created and a story is told.

The queen's beloved Skye, Islay, painted life-size, sits up, begging. His bright terrier eyes are fastened on a biscuit clutched by the macaw. But even a terrier knows better than to challenge such a big bird. Dignified and confident on his high perch, the macaw tilts his head as he slowly crumbles a piece of biscuit in his beak. The fluttering lovebirds, like Islay, will taste only the crumbs he scatters. At the base of the stand, Tilco, the black-and-tan spaniel, chews on a macaw feather. The puppy also has appropriated a wax-sealed envelope that his royal mistress gave the macaw to shred.

Bird scent is in the autumn air. Only the pointer's brown nose quivers. Once he locates the birds' hiding place, the dog will freeze. With muscles tensed and tail rigid, he will hold the point until his master catches up.

A short-haired coat of white, lightly flecked with liver, makes a pointer easy to follow. This handsome dog went afield with Theodore Roosevelt, the twenty-sixth president of the United States. A valued companion, his portrait was painted by J. M. Tracy, one of the great dog artists.

AARDVARK AND AARDWOLF

Aardvarks are bizarre, elusive, nocturnal termite- and ant-eating animals that are the only living member of the order Tubulidentata. Three of them are portrayed by Gustav Mützel in their open scrub and grassland habitat of Africa.

On zigzag course, snout to the ground and ears forward, an aardvark forages. Now and again it pauses, digs with its long, spoon-shaped, sharp-edged claws, sniffs, and then moves on. When ants or termites are located, the aardvark's long tongue, thin, round, and sticky, flicks in and out of the furrow it has dug. Ingested ants and termites go straight to a muscular, gizzardlike stomach to be ground up, because the tiny peg teeth that line either side of the aardvark's upper and lower jaws are of little use for chewing.

The aardwolf is a small, shy member of the hyena family. This pair has taken over an aardvark's den. The male has returned and now it is the female's turn to forage.

A specialist feeder, the aardwolf moves through the night with its large ears cupped forward, listening for the sound of termites feeding. Once located, termites are licked up with a long, mobile tongue covered with sticky saliva. As many as 200,000 termites are consumed in a night. When an aardwolf meets an intruder on its foraging route, the long hairs on its back and tail stand erect and give the animal an intimidating increase in body size.

This hand-colored lithograph from an 1869 volume is the work of John Gerrard Keulemans, a Dutch-born artist who preferred birds but occasionally painted mammals.

TWO ANIMALS WITH POUCHES

John Gould was celebrated in England as a bird artist whose books were richly illustrated with folio-size, hand-colored lithographic plates. When he traveled to Australia, it was to paint mammals as well as birds. He had the assistance of his artist wife, Eliza, and a lithographer, Henry Constantine Richter, who was adept at arranging botanical material and had an eye for composition.

Tree kangaroos (*below*) live in mountainous rain forests in northeastern Queensland. Evolving from a jumping to a tree-living existence, they developed arboreal adaptations. Their forelimbs are nearly as long as their hind legs. Tree kangaroos' forepaws have large, curved claws; their hind feet have broad, body-supporting claws. Thus equipped, tree kangaroos are agile climbers. The long tail is used for balance and as a brace. Their usual way of descent is to back down a tree.

Rembrandt Bugatti was born into an extraordinary family in Milan, Italy. His father was the famous furniture maker Carlo Bugatti, and his brother Ettore designed racing cars and manufactured the Bugatti automobile. As a small boy, Rembrandt learned metalworking in his father's studio, where sometimes he worked in clay. At nineteen, the young sculptor was exhibiting in the Paris gallery of A. A. Hebrard, the man who would cast almost all of Bugatti's bronzes.

Rembrandt Bugatti liked to sculpt groups of animals. This bronze encounter involves two kangaroos, but often his groups are of animals that contrast in size and shape. In all of the groups, each animal can stand by itself as a perfect study.

These big kangaroos have short forelimbs, long hind limbs for bounding, and heavy tails that function as props when the 'roos sit and as balances when they hop.

Bugatti completed a model in a single session, sometimes working all day in the zoo. If he was dissatisfied with the day's work, he destroyed or abandoned the piece. When he was satisfied, he made his own plaster model from plasteline. The plaster then went to his agent, the foundry owner A. A. Hebrard, to be cast by the lost-wax method.

RHINOCEROSES

Two Indian rhinoceroses, life-size, stand near the Bronx Zoo's elegant old elephant house that is now called Zoo Center. This is a fitting habitat for Bessie and Victoria, as both bronzes were modeled from a single rhino that lived in the building during the 1930s.

Victoria and Bessie, with their pendulous neck folds and wonderful blue-green hides, peer through the foliage. A closer look at Victoria reveals the knobby armor-plated body characteristic of her species. The single horn, which accounts for the scientific name *Rhinoceros unicornis*, also suggests a mythical connection with the unicorn.

Both grazers and browsers, Indian rhinos are fond of water, especially during the hot monsoon months. Wallowing cools them, discourages pesky flies, and provides a social time when as many as eight or nine rhinos share a wallow.

Victoria and Bessie, originally commissioned to flank the bronze doors of the Biological Laboratories at Harvard University, are the work of sculptor Katharine Lane Weems. The rhinos were modeled one at a time, Bessie, and months later, Victoria. A two-foot version was modeled. When it came to the four-foot clay enlargement, the sculptor had to renovate her studio, once a stable in Manchester, Massachusetts. The flooring had to be tested to be sure it would support a clay rhino's weight. And a huge new door had to be installed for Bessie's removal. Each rhino required a plaster piece mold of twenty-four parts, for which some twenty-three 100-pound bags of plaster were used. Then, one by one, the rhinos were transported to the foundry for sand casting.

Black rhinoceroses (*below*) stand resting in the midday African sun. Oxpeckers, or tick birds, cling to their cracked hides, searching for parasites and pecking at blood-encrusted sores. Being nearsighted, rhinos rely on tick birds as sentries. When the birds chirr in alarm, rhinos wheel and trot off, heads high and tails curled over their backs.

Ugo Mochi used black paper, a single sheet, and his small lithographer's knife to portray these rhinos, interpreting the massive forms of the male and female and the outline of the small calf with accuracy and sculptural simplicity.

The newborn calf stays close to its mother. When she moves, it will follow on her heels. Its horn is only a small nasal nubbin. The long horns of the adult rhinos, used in jousting matches, are composed of fibrous hairlike material and shaped by rubbing on termite mounds. Because the horn has only a thick-skin attachment, it is readily removed. The demand for horns in Arab and Asian countries, as dagger handles and for medicinal purposes, has sadly diminished the number of black rhinos.

An Indian rhino (*above*) is the subject of a drawing by the French artist Jean-Baptiste Oudry, who saw the "Dutch" rhinoceros when she came to Paris in 1749. Oudry was the official animal painter to the court of Louis XV.

Jungfer Clara (Miss Clara) was captured with snares in the northeast Indian state of Assam as a small calf. She was presented to a Dutch East India Company official in Bengal and enjoyed the run of the downstairs of his spacious house. After a few years the rhino outgrew her welcome. She was acquired by a Dutch sea captain, Douwe Mout van der Meer, and aboard his ship sailed for Holland. That is why Clara, the fifth rhinoceros to be seen in Europe, is called the "Dutch" rhinoceros.

For sixteen years Clara traveled about Europe, riding in a sturdy wagon, and accompanied by Douwe Mout and a retinue that included the wagon driver, her keeper, a clerk who arranged for the rhino's public appearances and distributed posters, and a ticket seller. Clara died in London at the age of twenty-one.

RACCOONS AND RELATIVES

A Central American tropical forest scene (*below*), perhaps by Gustav Mützel, comes from an 1883 edition of Brehm's *Thierleben*. White-nosed coatis, two females and a cub, search for insects and other small prey. Snuffling and probing with their rubbery noses, they investigate a vine-covered branch, relying on their strong clawed forepaws to extricate their finds.

Coatis, unlike their raccoon relatives, are active in the daytime. They are agile climbers. But mostly they forage on the ground, poking through the leaf litter with their mobile snouts, and carrying their long ringed tails high over their backs.

Coatis are social. Females, with their young, live in bands. Coatimundi, a word that means "lone coati," refers to the much larger male coati, who spends much of his time by himself.

The mountains of China's Sichuan Province, where bamboo forms thickets and rhododendrons are draped with beards of lichen, is panda habitat. There the ranges of the two pandas overlap. The bearlike giant panda is a specialist, feeding almost entirely on bamboo. The raccoonlike red panda supplements bamboo with buds and berries and an occasional mouse or nestling bird.

Arthur deCarle Sowerby was a capable artist and the son, grandson, and great-grandson of Sowerbys who were all noted illustrators of natural history subjects. He lived in China, where he founded the Shanghai Natural History Museum. Sowerby painted this charming watercolor (*above*) to accompany "The Pandas or Cat-bears," an article he published in the *China Journal*.

At nightfall on a spring evening, a raccoon interrupts his quest for crayfish and frogs to peer up at a big brown bat foraging for insects over the pond.

The raccoon is adapted for night life. Round, dark eyes that have an almost cone-shaped cornea gather and absorb the available light. Relying as it does on sense of touch, a raccoon has good close-up vision, but rather poor distance vision. Perhaps the raccoon heard the bat over the pond before he looked up to watch its fluttering flight.

Charles Livingston Bull was a highly successful illustrator who loved animals. He observed them with the keen eye of a naturalist, but his portrayal of them was never dispassionate. He combined his own deep feeling for the natural world with a superb sense of design. In spareness of detail and elegance of line, Bull's work owes a stylistic debt to the art of the Japanese print. In this nocturnal scene, which reveals the artist's sensitivity, there is balance, but not symmetry. The emphasis is on line and composition. There is a flatness of space. And for decorative effect the bat's left wing is cropped.

GIRAFFES AND OKAPI

In 1826 Mehemet Ali, pasha of Egypt, obtained two young giraffes that had been raised by Arabs in the Nubian desert. Strapped onto the backs of camels, the small giraffes endured a forty-five-day journey to Cairo. Then they were ferried down the Nile to Alexandria. From there the larger male giraffe, intended as a gift for Charles X of France, departed for Marseilles.

The female giraffe was shipped to Malta and, because she was travel-weary, kept there for six months. Then, aboard the *Penelope*, she sailed on to London, arriving at Waterloo Bridge on August 11, 1827. Edward Cross, proprietor of the menagerie at Exeter Change, took charge of her.

She was lodged in a nearby warehouse and then conveyed to Windsor. This is the giraffe presented to George IV. The king was reported to be "greatly pleased with the care which had been taken to bring the giraffe into his presence in fine order."

When Jacques-Laurent Agasse came with Mr. Cross to see the giraffe, the king commissioned the artist to paint his new acquisition. Agasse painted his animals with sensitivity and in luminous landscapes. The giraffe, in her Sandpit Gate paddock in Windsor Great Park, lowers her long neck. She is tempted by the tub of milk held by her two Arab keepers. A man in top hat and frock coat, presumed to be the pasha's European agent, looks on. Resting near the high board fence are the cows that supplied milk for the young giraffe.

Agasse painted with accuracy the quadrangular chestnut spots on buff-white body that are characteristic of the Nubian giraffe, a subspecies found in the Sudan. He also caught the gentle, even demure, nature of the young giraffe, gazing down on her attendants.

George IV grew very fond of his giraffe. He retained the services of Mr. Cross to insure her proper care. Sadly, the giraffe never fully recovered from her long journey to England. When she became unable to stand, the king ordered a pulley constructed to get the giraffe onto her feet. Two years after her arrival, the king's giraffe died.

This lithograph was made from a watercolor sketch by the okapi's discoverer, Sir Harry Johnston, a British explorer and colonial official with an interest in natural history. Johnston's quest to see the elusive "horselike, two-toed, striped animal" that the Pygmies said lived deep in the Congo forest was unsuccessful. However, he later was sent a skin and two skulls.

A watercolor sketch was done from these specimens and depicted the okapi as Johnston imagined it would look in life. He packed the sketch with the skin and skulls and shipped the box to the Zoological Society in London. Accompanying an account of the okapi's discovery and a description of the animal in the 1901 edition of the society's *Proceedings* is a hand-colored lithographic plate. It is the work of the Dutch-born artist and lithographer Joseph Smit, who illustrated many natural history books in England.

ELEPHANTS

J ust before giving birth to her calf, an elephant leaves her family unit, a group that consists of a wise old matriarch and one or two other cows, her daughters or sisters, and their calves.

The close bond between elephant cow and calf is evident in a life-size sculpture at the Philadelphia Zoo carved from a single piece of granite by Heinz Warneke.

So content appears the mother elephant that on a hot day it seems she might cool herself by fanning her huge ears. The calf has just suckled, its small trunk upturned so that its mouth could reach one of the two teats between the mother's forelegs. With her trunk the cow fondles her sleepy baby. The calf seems about to flop down for a nap in the shade of its mother.

In 1657 a traveling menagerie came to Amsterdam. Among those who came to see the animals was the famous painter Rembrandt van Rijn, who made numerous sketches of elephants and lions. His free-flowing lines suggest this patient elephant's wrinkled hide. With shuffling hind foot and curled trunk, the elephant looks about for more hay.

In Africa after the rains have come and gone, the long dry season causes grasses to wither and die. Then elephants feed on woody parts of shrubs and strip bark from trees. This big bull elephant has pushed over a tree. He stands with huge, rounded forefeet on the tree's trunk and pulls off a branch. The ripping of wood is almost audible and the gentle flapping of a large leathery ear almost visible.

When Ugo Mochi cut out his animals in paper, black on white, accuracy was essential. The outline of this big bull is both sculptural and dynamic.

As a young artist, Dame Laura Knight found inspiration for many of her paintings in the circus. During the early 1930s, as "official artist," she lived and moved about England with Carmo's Circus. "The circus," she wrote, "held my whole interest. I was there all day; I could leave it only to go back to sleep."

Laura Knight painted circus performers, clowns wistfully awaiting their turn in the ring, and bareback riders on their big leopard-spotted horses called *Knapstruppers*, which more than once knocked over her easel and spilled her paints as they cantered out of the ring. But the quiet moments out of the spotlights also attracted the artist.

No circus is without at least one Asian elephant. In this sensitively painted watercolor, the elephant Mary, tethered by a foot chain to a tent pole, feeds on a flake of hay near her Shetland-pony companions.

This small bronze African elephant, full of spirit and motion, is known as *Running Elephant*. With swinging trunk, flying ears and tail, it "moves" at the running walk that is the elephant's only fast gait.

Because of their immense body size, elephants require the support of at least one front and one hind leg. So they cannot trot, gallop, or jump. The running walk, covering five to seven miles in an hour, can be maintained for several hours.

Antoine-Louis Barye, a leading romantic sculptor, became the founder of a nineteenth-century French school of sculptors. After a critic dismissed the artist as *un animalier*, the epithet was taken up by a small but flourishing group of artists who specialized in modeling and carving animals. They called themselves *les animaliers*.

Barye was a regular zoo visitor, spending days in the Jardin des Plantes, sketching from life and observing animals. When an animal died, he was summoned by his keeper friends and came quickly to make measurements of its body. Working in the zoo was a way of life for Barye. Years after acquiring the patronage of two prosperous American art collectors, the successful sculptor still could be found in the zoo. When one of the patrons, William Walters of Baltimore, visited Barye's studio, he was told by Madame Barye, "Ah, Monsieur, there is no use calling . . . a new tiger has arrived from Bengal; until its wildness has gone—no Monsieur Barye."

Barye's intense interest in each of his animals carried through to overseeing every step of the casting process, from model to mold-making, to casting, chasing, and finally to patinating the bronze. His *Running Elephant* was sand cast in two pieces. Barye himself did much of the after-work on his animals: chiseling, chasing, filing, pointing up details, and polishing and reworking surfaces to give life to the bronze. The bases were cast separately and then attached mechanically to the animals.

ARCTIC ANIMALS

A muskox bull has a heavy, long-haired coat and a bold boss of horns across his brow. Carved in olivine, this one came from Iqaluit on Baffin Island in the Canadian Arctic. His owner, Leo J. Hickey, whose research interests take him every summer to the Far North, describes hours spent "watching old bulls standing nearly motionless on high hills and cliff edges . . . with the wind blowing cold right off the glacier to billow their stiff skirts," just as the artist Nooveya Ipeelie has shown in stone.

Called *oomingmak,* or "bearded one," by the Inuit, the muskox is the largest of the goat antelopes, a curious group of hoofed mammals that are stocky in build and gregarious by nature. Curved horns grow from a thick, bony shield that protects the muskox's forehead in horn-crashing contests between bulls. A massive coat of long, dark-brown guard hairs forms a beard and long skirts that reach to the white ankles. Beneath this snow-shedding coat is a dense insulating layer of fine, light-brown hair. When muskoxen wheel in alarm and gallop off in hairy confusion, they seem to flow over the tundra, their dark backs rising and falling and long hair blowing.

A muskox herd, consisting of as many as ten or more animals, includes a lead bull, several younger bulls, and cows with their calves.

In the early 1950s James Houston, an authority on the Far North, brought the first Inuit sculpture to the United States. An artist himself, Houston admired the Inuit carvers' understanding of anatomy, which he said is "like a butcher's." In the best of their carvings the animal's spirit is also captured, usually in stone, but sometimes in ivory, bone, or antler.

This handsome walrus (*above*) that belongs to James and Alice Houston was carved in olivine by the Inuit artist Oshaweetuk. The defender of a family of three females and their calves, the walrus keeps watch, with bloodshot eyes, for the approach of rival bulls or men in boats.

From bristly mustache to tail, a big male walrus measures nearly twelve feet. His oarlike front flippers are two feet long. The slightly smaller hind flippers turn forward, so that a walrus can get up on its limbs and move freely on land.

A thick layer of fat and tough leathery skin cover the walrus. Tusks, elongated upper canine teeth, are weapons for defense. Enamel-tipped when they erupt, they are entirely dentin (ivory). Tusks also are useful for hooking onto an ice floe when hauling out of the water, for breaking through ice, and sometimes for killing a seal.

ZEBRAS

Staked by a tether attached to the noseband of her bridle, a zebra mare stands quietly in this small painting, a Mughal miniature. The artist, Ustad Mansur, was prominent in the Mughal school of painting of seventeenth-century India. The Mughals, who invaded India, established a powerful dynasty that was essentially Persian. The Indian painters who became court artists were influenced by Persian techniques. Ignoring shading and perspective, they drew elegant lines and created brilliant mosaics of pure colors.

Mughal painting flourished during the reign of Jahangir, who had a deep interest in the natural world and an artist's eye for the beauty of ani-

mals. Whenever and wherever he traveled, Jahangir included artists in his cavalcade of attendants mounted on horses and elephants. The artists were to record what was seen, in particular any rare animals. Mansur did many sensitive and detailed animal studies and was designated the chief animal portraitist.

The zebra's meticulously painted stripe pattern is that of a plains zebra. Mansur portrayed the zebra with subtlety of line and luminous color. Her attitude suggests that she was docile, even domesticated. Yet Mansur observed the zebra with empathy and the respect that is due a wild animal.

ANTELOPES

Rembrandt Bugatti loved animals for their pure and simple goodness. He ended a letter home "embrace everyone—and all the animals because I love them too. They are my faithful friends." The sculptor devoted his life to animals, working long hours in the Paris zoo and later in the Antwerp zoo, where artists were encouraged and could find, for their models, many unusual animals.

Of all his groups of animals, it is this kudu family (*below*) that reveals the depth of Bugatti's empathy. At first glance it is apparent that the kudu cow is not well. Her head hangs dejectedly and her coat is scruffy. The calf shows concern, nuzzling its mother's neck. Even the bull kudu is attentive. The heavy cast on the mother kudu's hind leg tells the story. The slim-limbed antelope has broken her leg. The antelopes are portrayed with tenderness, yet without sentimentalism.

One of the spiral-horned antelopes, kudus are slender in build and have long, narrow faces. They live in hilly thicket and woodland areas of Africa. There, the six to ten vertical white stripes on their sandy gray bodies simulate sunlight streaking through twigs and branches and conceal these shy antelopes. Foliage gleaners, kudus feed on fruits, seed pods, flowers, bark, and tubers, as well as leaves.

Indian miniature paintings of the early 1600s, full of rhythm and vitality, include all kinds of animals, intimately portrayed. This blackbuck, shown with his keeper, may have belonged to the Mughal emperor Jahangir. The antelope's importance is indicated by the fact that, in proportion to the keeper, he is painted nearly twice his actual size. The artist Manohar suggests a feeling of trust between antelope and man.

The blackbuck, graceful and slender, has long legs, a long neck, and a sheeplike muzzle. It belongs to the group of antelopes called gazelles. Only the male is black, or very dark brown; females are fawn-colored. And only the male has horns, which are ringed and twisted in as many as five turns. With horn displays and threat gestures, the male establishes dominance.

Most blackbuck herds, of five to fifty, are harems, a male and his females with their young. When alarmed by a predator, the blackbuck leaps high into the air, signaling danger. The herd reacts. The antelopes explode in a stiff-legged gait called pronking, or stotting, and with each bound land with all four hooves together, confusing the predator. Safety lies in speed, and the herd gallops off.

Few enemies except the cheetah, once trained for the chase, can overtake the fleet blackbuck.

When the ship *Slaney* docked at Woolwich in June of 1827 there were two white-tailed gnus aboard. The animal dealer Edward Cross arranged for the transport of these large antelopes to Windsor Great Park and at once had a farrier trim their overgrown hooves. Seven months later a third gnu joined the royal menagerie and George IV decided to commission this painting by Jacques-Laurent Agasse.

The king's three gnus occupy the foreground of the painting. In the background other gnus rest, graze, trot, canter, and buck. Two males contest territory by horn-shoving.

In the distance Agasse painted in a herd of quaggas, the partly striped, white-tailed equids that the artist knew were the gnus' grazing companions on the South African veld.

The white-tailed gnu, also called the black wildebeest, has a large head, humped shoulders, a bearded throat, a handsome mane, a tuft of hair between its forelegs, and a long, white tail that almost sweeps the ground. A facial brush of stiff, upward-growing hair gives the gentle gnu a rather ferocious appearance.

CATS

An "eager Cockney cat" is art historian Kenneth Clark's description of what he termed "perhaps the best cat in art." Intent on a frightened, fluttering finch, the small gray tiger-striped cat, ears and vibrissae (whiskers) forward and mouth open, anticipates a "kill" and sinks its sharp claws into the back of a chair.

This wonderfully observed cat is seen in detail from a large canvas by William Hogarth, well known for his portrayals of eighteenth-century English life. The painting is a group portrait of the four Graham children, who seem quite unaware of their cat's stalk.

Swiss-born Théophile-Alexandre Steinlen celebrated the cat in illustrations for books and magazines, advertisements, posters, and prints. He lived in a cat-filled house in the Montmartre section of Paris. With uncanny feline understanding, he portrayed cats in all their shapes, colors, moods, and poses. Even in his scenes of Parisian life, Steinlen found space and excuse to include cats.

In this cover for *Des Chats* ("Some Cats"), a book of the artist's own "stories without words," Colette, his small daughter, holds a bowl of milk for six hungry cats, all meowing. A black cat pushes against the little girl's skirt, while the tiger cat claws at her waist.

A romantic realist, the painter Eugène Delacroix favored tigers and lions as wild-animal subjects. He painted them battling snakes, attacking Arabian horses, fighting men, or by themselves, but always in imaginary landscapes. Even though this tiger is resting, its powerful, striped form gives the impression of tremendous feline energy.

Carl Rungius liked best to paint the animals of the Canadian Rockies. Some, like this bobcat, were seen near his Banff studio, called the Paintbox. Others were sketched and painted on pack trips through the mountains.

Rungius's bobcat, being a mountain dweller, is large and heavy-bodied. He has dark, inch-long ear tufts. Cheek fur forms muttonchops that give width to his face. His thick, reddish-brown fur, marbled and spotted with black, blends in among the boulders, brush, and downed timber of the shadowy forest. He moves through his five-square-mile home range, making seasonal use of various convenient den sites and hiding places.

The bobcat has spent the day stretched out on a rock ledge in the warm sun. Now, at dusk, he stirs. Downslope there are varying hares hopping about among the willows. If the bobcat's stalk-and-pounce hunting technique is successful, he will have himself a hare for supper.

PRIMATES

Of all the portraits of her pets by Sir Edwin Landseer, Queen Victoria favored the small painting known as "the pineapple monkeys." In fact, she was so fond of the painting that once, when it had been kept too long by the artist, a dispatch from Buckingham Palace advised Landseer that the queen would be pleased to have returned "the pine apple [sic] Monkeys, one of the most beautiful of your smaller pieces."

Queen Victoria's pets were two kinds of tufted-ear marmosets, a black tufted-ear marmoset and a white tufted-ear marmoset. The two tiny South American primates peer anxiously at the wasp that has interrupted their feeding on pineapple and nuts. What makes the painting so appealing is the contrast in size (between marmosets and pineapple and between marmosets and wasp), the riot of curves (of tails, leaves of the pineapple, edge of the plate, and swirl pattern of the background), and the wonderful, rich colors.

Marmosets run along branches and make vertical cling-and-leap jumps from tree to tree in their rain-forest habitat. They feed on fruits and insects and, with specialized lower jaw and teeth, bite small holes in tree bark to consume sap, sometimes riddling a favorite tree with their bite holes.

From *The Royal Natural History* comes this charming wood engraving (*below*) of small, owllike night monkeys by Friedrich Specht, a German-born artist who probably saw the monkeys in the London Zoo. Night monkeys are the only truly nocturnal monkeys. Like all nocturnal mammals, they have very large eyes that enable them to see well at low light levels. By being nocturnal, night monkeys avoid eagles, hawks, and large monkeys, all efficient daytime hunters.

In forests of South America night monkeys travel in family groups of two to five. Preferring densely forested areas with many vines, they feed on fruits, insects, flower nectar, and an occasional lizard or nestling bird. A group may occupy a single fruit tree for much of the night, moving about to feed or sitting quietly.

On moonlit nights the low, resonant, hooting calls of the males carry through the forest, proclaiming territories and luring mates. When the little monkeys fight, it is one family against another, and war whoops sound. Usually the home team wins and the interlopers move off through the trees.

Working from life in the zoo, Rembrandt Bugatti must have been challenged by this male baboon (*above*), which asserts his dominance by standing tall on his forelimbs. A hamadryas baboon, whose descriptive name comes from classical mythology and means "tree nymph," the sculptor's model is descended from the sacred baboons of the ancient Egyptians.

Largest of the monkeys, the baboon is a ground walker. It strides with shoulders higher than hips because of lengthened arm bones and the additional lift of its palms. Its tail is carried in a curve. Now and again the baboon pauses. Using one hand to support its front end, it reaches with the stubby calloused fingers of its free hand to pluck grass, or dig for a root or a beetle larva.

The face and rump of the hamadryas baboon are bareskinned and red. Long silver-gray fur forms a warm cape for living in the harsh rocky desert habitat of northeastern Africa. The cape may also serve for status among these highly social animals, which live in large groups, called troops, of as many as two hundred baboons.

A troop consists of smaller bands (of fifty or more) that, because sleeping sites are scarce, return at dusk to the same cliff. Within each band are several clans, made up of two or three families, each led by an adult male, like this bronze baboon, with several females and their offspring.

HORSES

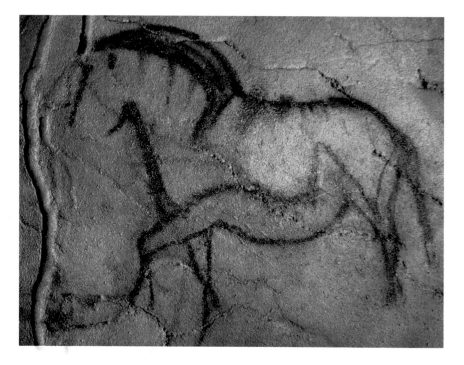

Ever since human beings began to draw, paint, engrave, model, and carve, animals have been their subjects. In fact, animals in art mark the beginning of *all* art. The first animal artists were prehistoric peoples who lived 12,000 to 14,000 years ago. Their animals in art—bison, ibex, mammoths, and horses—decorate the craggy walls, narrow passages, and low ceilings of caves in southern France and northern Spain.

Three basic colors made up the cave-painters' palette: black, red, and yellow. Carbon and manganese, clay ocher, and iron oxide, dug from the ground near the caves and ground to powder between slabs of stone, were mixed with animal fat,

bone marrow, or vegetable oils to make paints and crayonlike drawing sticks. Where bulges in the cave wall suggested body shape, the artist skillfully made use of them to model animals in relief.

This black horse from Le Portel in Ariège, France, drawn with sureness of hand and superb economy of line, is perfectly proportioned and full of animation.

Jean Vertut, who photographed the horse during the arduous fifteen-year project of recording the treasures of prehistoric art, devised special equipment to support his cameras, lights, and batteries so that he could film the animals at close range and from different angles.

A mutual fondness for animals was the basis of the friendship between Jacob Bell, the owner of a pharmaceutical company, and the painter Sir Edwin Landseer. Bell's animals, including his favorite bay mare and his bloodhounds, often were borrowed as models.

For ten years Bell had wanted a painting of his bay mare, Old Betty. He had hoped to have her portrayed with a foal. But by 1844, when Landseer at last got around to the commission, the mare had produced two foals, and both of them were grown. So the artist decided on a shoeing scene.

The gentle mare turns to watch the farrier. Her companions, the bloodhound Laura and a patient donkey, are attentive. Laura slobbers in anticipation. Like most dogs, she delights in the taste and chewing texture of hoof trimmings. The donkey, whose feet sometimes require trimming, but never shoeing, is curious about the hiss and smell of smoke and burning hoof as the hot shoe is set.

Old Betty stands quietly without a halter and shank because she pulled back and broke her halter whenever she was tied. Her right forefoot takes very little of her weight. Like many older horses, Bell's mare probably had navicular disease, an inflammation of a small bone in the hoof.

The bay mare's coat gleams in the summer sunlight that slants through the stable door, and the skin ripples on her sleek rump.

Even as a small child, Rosa Bonheur was involved with animals. Her mother took her to see cows and horses and encouraged her to draw them. Her father, an artist, let her keep rabbits, chickens, ducks, and even a goat in his studio. There Rosa, with her sister and two brothers, worked happily during evening drawing sessions.

The young artist soon wanted to know more about animal form. "One must know what is under their skin. Otherwise your animal will look like a mat rather than a tiger." Rosa Bonheur's visits to a local slaughterhouse created a stir. Undaunted, she obtained a certificate from the Paris police that allowed her to dress as a man. "Thus," she wrote, "I was taken for a young lad and unmolested."

Rosa Bonheur also frequented the horse market at the boulevard de L'Hôpital, where she watched horses that reminded her of the lithographs of horses by the romantic painter Théo-dore Géricault that she had seen in the studio of her sculptor friend Mêne. Rosa admired Géricault's horses, especially "the heavy rounded majesty of his work horses." She made many drawings of the Percherons and other horses and soon was at work on an enormous canvas.

The Horse Fair was exhibited in the salon of 1853, where it drew acclaim from critics and from a public amazed by the painting's immense size and by the artist's dramatic depiction of a familiar scene. The disposition of the massed horses (some trotting with tremendous impulsion and pulling against their bits, others rearing), the tensions between the horses and the men trying to control them, and the riders' positions echo the influence of Géricault. The big horses are of many colors—gray, roan, chestnut, and brown. The artist skillfully used bright accents of blue and scarlet. In the distance is the dome of the hospital, for which the boulevard was named.

In 1761 George Stubbs painted this life-size portrait (*right*) of the English Thoroughbred Whistlejacket. With hind legs deeply flexed, the stallion executes a *levade*, an equine pose often used in monuments, as well as in portraits. His owner, the second marquis of Rockingham, intended that King George III should be mounted on the splendid chestnut. The royal rider and a landscape background were to have been painted by other artists.

Lord Rockingham may have been so delighted by what Stubbs achieved that he decided Whistlejacket should remain riderless. Or, his decision may have been influenced by a political falling-out with the king. Or, by the stallion's unruly temperament. The artist's friend Ozias Humphry wrote of the last sitting for the chestnut's portrait:

> Stubbs put his work in a good light and observed its effect, as artists do. . . . [Suddenly] the boy who was leading Whistlejacket up and down, called out . . . and turning Stubbs saw the horse staring at his own portrait and quivering with rage. He sprang forward to attack it, rearing and lifting the boy off his legs.

Stubbs, quick to protect his painting, pummeled the stallion with his palette.

For three years prior to this commission, Stubbs, who had no formal training as a painter, lived in a remote farmhouse in Lincolnshire, near the village of Horkstow, where, with the help of his lifelong companion Mary Spencer, he dissected and made detailed drawings of horses. A

very large man of prodigious strength, Stubbs used a tackle to hoist a horse carcass into lifelike positions. Then it hung for weeks at a time, until the stench became unbearable, as the artist flayed it to reveal muscles, blood vessels, and skeletal parts. His detailed drawings were the basis for the plates in *The Anatomy of the Horse*, published in 1766.

Herbert Haseltine modeled and carved horses of all kinds—race horses, hunters, polo ponies, and giant draft horses. As a sculptor he maintained that "sculpture should be closely associated with the choice of beautiful materials· and patinas," a theory handsomely translated in this gold-plated Suffolk punch stallion (*left*), mane and tail braided with lapis lazuli, that flexes his neck and rolls his eyes of onyx and ivory.

Sudbourne Premier was a prized horse. Like all Suffolk punch horses he was a chestnut. No other color is allowed for the breed, which originated in England's county of Suffolk. Unlike most of the other English draft breeds, which have long-haired fetlocks, the Suffolk Punch is "clean legged." Short legs and round-bodied conformation make the horse a powerful puller.

From an exhibition of the Society of French Animal Portrayers, most of whom worked in Paris, often in the zoo, during the early 1900s, comes a powerfully carved Przewalski horse (*above*). Although the stallion is somewhat stylized, the characteristics of this small, stocky Mongolian wild horse, the ancestor of the domestic horse, are evident. The neck is topped by a dark, upright mane; the tail is long and thick, brushy over the dock; dark stockings mark the lower legs; the head is large in proportion to the body; and the muzzle is mealy colored. A beard suggests that the sculptor observed the horse in winter. Even its yellowish-brown coat color, fading to yellowish white on the belly, is indicated.

This unique horse, named for a Russian explorer, is gone from the wild. Some one thousand of these genetically distinct horses, all of them descended from thirteen wild horses captured at the turn of the century, live in zoos and reserves around the world.

For Edgar Degas there was an important difference between seeing a horse and seeing it while modeling it. Modeling gave him an understanding of body mass, the mechanism of movement, the balance, and the play between convex and concave contours. Degas began to model horses after seeing Eadweard Muybridge's *Animal Locomotion*, a book of photographs of animals in motion that was published in 1887.

A painter whose passions were the ballet and the racetrack, Degas taught himself to model dancers and horses. When a limb he was sculpting needed support, Degas simply propped it up with a match. His improvised armatures often collapsed. Nevertheless, the artist, who had done many studies of women bathing, became so involved with modeling horses and capturing in wax all their movements that he exclaimed to a friend: "I haven't yet done enough horses. The women must wait in their tubs."

Degas modeled his horses at the walk, trot, canter, and gallop. Others prance nervously, balk, and rear in fear. A few of the horses were cast in plaster during the artist's lifetime. The others that survived were found crumbling in his studio and were cast in bronze after his death. There are thirteen of these race horses. Here (*below*) is one of them.

Turn of head and slackened jaw suggest that this horse, reluctantly slowing to a trot after the excitement of a gallop on the track, pulls against the hold of an invisible jockey.

Perhaps the most charming of the horse paintings by Jacques-Laurent Agasse is this one of a beautiful gray, whose blanket has been removed to give the owner, the Honorable Henry Wellesley, a better look at his prized stallion.

The gray was one of two horses imported by Lord Wellesley in 1803, described as exceptionally handsome and said to be "Persian or Syrian, with a considerable admixture of Arabian blood." The shah of Persia may have advised Lord Wellesley, who was the youngest brother of the Duke of Wellington, in his selection of the gray and a chestnut. A horse of substance and power, the gray ran and won for Lord Wellesley on Newmarket Heath, where English Thoroughbreds have raced since the early seventeenth century.

Agasse, like Stubbs, had dissected and studied the anatomy of the horse. By 1809, when this portrait was commissioned, Lord Wellesley's gray was much in demand as a stud. Agasse's painting is in fact a stud portrait. The horse's conformation, condition, and even his gentle manners are suggested. The gray appears alive, with rippling muscles and shimmering coat. The painting itself reflects the artist's fine understanding of the horse and the affection he felt for his subject.

SOME SMALL ANIMALS

The Scottish artist Joseph Crawhall was said to have been more at ease with the animals he knew and loved than he was with human beings. His empathy with these two Dutch rabbits is evident.

One of the black-and-white rabbits nibbles a carrot. Its companion, head turned and ears cocked, is ready to bolt for cover at the back of the hutch. With few brush strokes, Crawhall perfectly outlined the rabbits' bodies and captured their personalities in watercolor.

Archibald Thorburn was a Scotsman who relied on closely observing, and even handling, the small mammals he painted. Often he captured his models and kept them for a short time. He also knew their habits and almost always painted them with suitable scenery.

Even in this watercolor sketch of a bat, with its short, stumpy, black-whiskered face, the artist suggests habitat, the opening of a tree hole. By day the cavity is the small bat's roosting place. When darkness comes, the bat emerges to flit through tree branches, across meadows, and over ponds in pursuit of insects.

The flying squirrel is a small goblin of the night with very large, dark eyes, rimmed with black; soft brownish-gray fur; long, sensitive vibrissae (whiskers); a small, slightly upturned nose; and a featherlike tail. It is actually a glider rather than a flier. Lateral skin folds, defined with black fur, extend between its wrists and ankles.

When the squirrel launches from a high branch, its four legs spread to extend the skin folds, increasing the surface of its light, flattened body. Like a miniature flying carpet, the squirrel sails through the air. Its tail functions as a rudder to control the glide. Thirty feet away, low on a tree trunk, the squirrel lands head up, with a soft plop, and dashes up the tree to gain altitude for another glide.

Dorothy Lathrop lived in northwestern Connecticut, sharing a studio with her sculptor sister, Gertrude Lathrop. So it is likely that the flying squirrel she knew was the northern flying squirrel, the larger of two species, that prefers to live in stands of conifers (cone-bearing trees) or in a mixed forest of conifers and hardwoods.

Active through the winter, this flying squirrel is about to leap from a snow-laden pine branch. Its landing may make a small, four-pawed sitzmark in the snow. Or, if the glide is long and descent is gradual, a foot-long dragmark will record its landing. Scampering over the snow, the flying squirrel will forage for its favorite food, the fungi that grow around the roots of trees and beneath fallen logs.

51

SHEEP AND A CALF

Ritish sculptor Henry Moore had a fondness for sheep. Using a black ballpoint pen, he filled his sketchbook with drawings of the sheep that grazed the fields surrounding his studio.

In his sculpture, a favorite theme was the large form related to the small and protecting it. So he delighted in the lambing season, when he could sketch the interacting forms of ewes and their lambs. He caught this suckling lamb's vigorous, impatient pushing against the ewe.

The sheep themselves admired Moore as a sculptor: "There is," he wrote, "one big sculpture of mine that I call *Sheep Piece* because I placed it in a field and the sheep enjoyed it and the lambs played around it."

portrait sculptor of international renown, Jo Davidson also could model animals. An overturned bucket suggests this calf has just been fed. The calf, beautifully balanced on three legs, reaches its slim neck with a hind hoof. Closed eyes and drooped ears suggest the pleasure of a good scratching.

THE ILLUSTRATIONS

page ii Abu'l-Hasan (or Abu'l-Hasan and Mansur): *The Chenar Tree*, ca. 1610. Mughal miniature painting. Opaque watercolor on paper, 14½ × 8⅞ inches. By permission of the Oriental and India Office Collections (British Library). Photograph courtesy of The Metropolitan Museum of Art.

page vii William D. Berry (1926–1979): *Raccoon*, ca. 1959. Opaque watercolor, 5 × 7 inches. Private collection. Reproduced by courtesy of Elizabeth Berry. Photograph by William K. Sacco.

page viii Wilhelm Kuhnert (1865–1926): *Wild Cat*. From *Thierleben der Erde*, vol. 1, by Wilhelm Haade and Wilhelm Kuhnert. Berlin: Verlag von Martin Oldenbourg, 1920.

page 2 *Rosa Bonheur's studio on the rue de l'Ouest*. Lithograph. From Edmond Texier, *Tableau de Paris*, Volume 2, 1853.

page 3 John Ballantyne, RSA (1815–1897): *Sir Edwin Landseer Sculpting His Lions*, ca. 1865. Oil on canvas. National Portrait Gallery, London.

page 4 *At the Antwerp Zoo in 1906*. Photograph of Rembrandt Bugatti (1884–1916). Courtesy of the Royal Zoological Society of Antwerp.

page 4 *At the Bronx Zoo*. Photograph of Ugo Mochi (1889–1977) by Sam Dunton, ca. 1950.

page 5 *The Sculptor at Work, 1908*. Photograph of A. Phimister Proctor (1860–?1950). © New York Zoological Society Photo.

page 6 Bruno Liljefors (1860–1939): *Foxes*, 1886. Oil on canvas, 28⅔ × 36½ inches. Courtesy of The Gothenburg Art Gallery (Göteborgs Konstmuseum), Sweden. Photograph by Ebbe Carlsson.

page 7 Pierre Jules Mêne (1810–1879): *Fox in a Snare*, ca. 1840–1845. Bronze, 3 × 5¼ × 2¼ inches. Private collection. Photograph by William K. Sacco.

page 7 Charles M. Russell (1864–1926): *Wolf*, 1915. Painted wax, grass, and plaster, 5¼ × 7⅝ × 4¼ inches. The Amon Carter Museum, Fort Worth. (1961:52).

page 8 Frederick G. R. Roth (1872–1944): *Polar Bear*. Statuette, bronze. The Metropolitan Museum of Art, Rogers Fund, 1906. (06.400).

page 9 Paul Manship (1885–1966): *Group of Bears*, cast in 1963. Bronze, 88 × 72 × 56 inches. The Metropolitan Museum of Art, Purchase, Sheila W. and Richard J. Schwartz Fund, in honor of Lewis I. Sharp, 1989.

(1989.19). Photograph by Jerry L. Thompson.

page 10 François Pompon (1855–1933): *Polar Bear (L'Ours Blanc)*, 1922. White marble on black marble base, 9⅜ × 19 inches. The Metropolitan Museum of Art, Edward C. Moore, Jr., Gift Fund, 1930. (30.123 ab).

page 11 *Figure of a Hippopotamus*. Egyptian (from the Tomb of the Steward Senbi at Meir), Twelfth Dynasty (ca. 1991–1786 B.C.) Ceramics (faience), 4⅜ × 7⅞ inches. The Metropolitan Museum of Art, Gift of Edward S. Harkness, 1917. (17.9.1).

page 11 Donald Richard Miller (1925–1989): *Mother and Child*, 1980. Bronze, 5¾ × 8 × 8½ inches. Courtesy of Harriet Phillips Miller.

page 12 Sir Edwin Landseer, RA (1803–1873): *The Sleeping Bloodhound*, by 1835. Oil on canvas, 39 × 49 inches. Courtesy of The Trustees of The Tate Gallery, London. Tate Gallery, London/Art Resource, New York.

page 13 Cecil Aldin (1870–1935): *Little Dog Riley*. Pastel. From *The Cecil Aldin Book*. New York: Charles Scribner's Sons, 1932. Reproduced by permission of the publisher. Photograph by William K. Sacco.

page 13 Paul Bransom (1885–1979): *Sunnybank Collie*, ca. 1927. Watercolor and charcoal on paper, 9 × 12 inches. Courtesy of Althea Bond, for the Estate of the Artist.

page 14 Sir Edwin Landseer, RA (1803–1873): *Macaw, Lovebirds, Terrier, and Spaniel Puppy, Belonging to Her Majesty*, 1839. Oil on canvas, 51¼ × 28 inches. Courtesy of The Royal Collection. Copyright reserved to Her Majesty Queen Elizabeth II.

page 15 J. M. Tracy (1844–1893): *Pointer*, ca. 1886. Oil on canvas, 12 × 20 inches. Collection of Alexander Fraser Draper. Photograph by William K. Sacco.

page 16 Gustav Mutzel (1839–1893): *Aardvark*. Wood engraving. From *The Royal Natural History*, vol. 3, by Richard Lydekker. London: Frederick Warne and Company, 1894–1895. Photograph by William K. Sacco.

page 16 John Gerrard Keulemans (1842–1912): *Aardwolf*. Lithograph, hand-colored. From *Proceedings of the Zoological Society, London*, 1869. Photograph by William K. Sacco.

page 17 John Gould (1804–1881) and Henry Constantine Richter: *Tree-kangaroo*. Lithograph, hand-colored. From *Monograph of the Macropodidae*, Part 2, 1842. Collection of B. Elizabeth Horner.

page 38 Eugène Delacroix (1798–1863): *Tigre Royale.* Lithograph, 7¼ × 23¹⁄₁₆ inches. Yale University Art Gallery, Gift of Ralph Kirkpatrick.

page 39 Carl Rungius (1869–1959): *Bay Lynx* (or Bobcat), ca. 1929. Oil on canvas. From "Carl Rungius, Artist, Naturalist, Sportsman" by Douglas Allen, Jr. In *The Conservationist* 40(2): 27, 1985. Photograph by William K. Sacco.

page 40 Charles F. Tunnicliffe, RA (1901–1979): *Cat and Kittens,* 1936. Wood engraving. Reproduced by kind permission, © The Tunnicliffe Trustees. From *Portrait of a Country Artist: C. F. Tunnicliffe RA* by Ian Niall. London: Victor Gollancz Ltd., 1985.

page 40 Josef Wolf (1820–1899) and Joseph Smit (1836–1929): *Felis caracal.* Lithograph, 18½ × 23¼ inches. From *A Monograph of the Felidae, or Family of the Cats* by Daniel Giraud Elliot, 1883. Photograph by William K. Sacco.

page 41 George Stubbs, ARA (1724–1806): *Cheetah and Stag with Two Indians* (detail), 1765. Oil on canvas, 71⅛ × 107⅝ inches. City of Manchester Art Galleries. Photograph by William K. Sacco.

page 42 Sir Edwin Landseer, RA (1803–1873): *A Pair of Brazilian Monkeys, the Property of Her Majesty* (also called *Brazilian Marmosets*), 1842. Oil on canvas, 12⅛ × 17¾ inches. Courtesy of The Royal Collection. Copyright reserved to Her Majesty Queen Elizabeth II.

page 43 Rembrandt Bugatti (1884–1916): *Hamadryas Baboon,* ca. 1910. Bronze, 17 × 17½ inches. From the collection of the John L. Wehle Gallery of Sporting Art, Genesee Country Museum, Mumford, New York. Photograph by John Danicic.

page 43 Friedrich Specht (1839–1909): *Night Monkeys.* Wood engraving. From *The Royal Natural History,* vol. 1, by Richard Lydekker. London: Frederick Warne and Company, 1894–1895. Photograph by William K. Sacco.

page 44 Artist unknown: *Horse from Le Portel,* Gallery 3. Paleolithic cave painting from Le Portel, Ariège, France. About 16 inches. Photograph by Jean Vertut, reproduced by permission of Mme. Yvonne Vertut.

page 45 Sir Edwin Landseer, RA (1803–1873): *Shoeing,* 1844. Oil on canvas, 56¹⁄₁₆ × 44 inches. The Trustees of The Tate Gallery, London. Tate Gallery, London/Art Resource, New York.

page 46 Rosa Bonheur (1822–1899): *The Horse Fair,* 1853–1855. Oil on canvas, 96¼ × 199½ inches. The Metropolitan Museum of Art, Gift of Cornelius Vanderbilt, 1887. (87.25).

page 47 George Stubbs, ARA (1724–1806): *Whistlejacket,* 1762. Oil on canvas, 115 × 97 inches. Reproduced by kind permission of the Trustees of the Rt. Hon. Olive, Countess Fitzwilliam's Chattels Settlement and the Lady Juliet de Chair. Photograph courtesy of the Paul Mellon Centre, London.

page 47 Herbert Haseltine (1877–1962): *Suffolk Punch Stallion: Sudbourne Premier* from the set *The Champion Animals of Great Britain,* 1924–1934. Bronze, plated with gold, lapis lazuli, ivory, and onyx, one-quarter life-size (21½ × 24½ × 6½ inches.). Virginia Museum of Fine Arts, the Paul Mellon Collection.

page 48 J. Piffard: *Przewalski Horse,* ca. 1918. Stone. From *Animals in Decoration and Sculpture* by Armand Dayot. Twenty-four plates. N.p., n.d.

page 48 Edgar Degas (1834–1917): *Horse with Head Lowered,* (No. 22, Set F) probably modeled 1870s, cast in 1919–1921. Bronze, 7⅛ × 10½ × 3¼ inches. Courtesy of the Sterling and Francine Clark Art Institute, Williamstown, Massachusetts.

page 49 Jacques-Laurent Agasse (1767–1849): *Portrait of the Grey Wellesley Arabian with His Owner and Groom in a Stable,* 1809. Oil on canvas, 33½ × 43⅜ inches. Private collection, by courtesy of Hildegard Fritz-Denneville Fine Arts, Ltd., London.

page 50 Joseph Crawhall (1861–1913): *Two Rabbits,* ca. 1893. Watercolor heightened with body color on paper, 11½ × 15 inches. The Burrell Collection, Glasgow Museums and Art Galleries.

page 50 Archibald Thorburn (1860–1935): *Whiskered Bat,* 1920. Watercolor on paper. Yale University, Beinecke Rare Book and Manuscript Library, the W. R. Coe Collection.

page 51 Dorothy P. Lathrop (1891–1980): *Pixie, a Flying Squirrel.* Wood engraving. From *Animal Drawing and Painting* by Walter J. Wilwerding. New York: Dover Publications, 1966. Reproduced by permission of the publisher. Photograph by William K. Sacco.

page 52 Henry Moore (1898–1986): *Sheep with Lamb,* 1972. Black ballpoint pen, crayon, and wash, 8¼ × 9⅞ inches. From *Sheep Sketchbook* by Henry Moore. New York: Thames and Hudson, 1980. Reproduced by kind permission of the Henry Moore Foundation. Photograph by William K. Sacco.

page 52 Jo Davidson (1883–1952): *Calf.* Plaster, 7½ × 8½ × 4¾ inches. Private collection. Photograph by William K. Sacco.

page 56 Charles F. Tunnicliffe, RA (1901–1979). *The Shire Stallion,* ca. 1941. Wood engraving. Reproduced by kind permission, © The Tunnicliffe Trustees. From *My Country Book* by C. F. Tunnicliffe. London: The Studio, 1947.

INDEX OF ARTISTS